Harvard Business Review

CLASSICS

1604-01

CONTROL IN AN AGE
OF EMPOWERMENT

Robert Simons

Harvard Business Press
Boston, Massachusetts

12 11 10 09 08   5 4 3 2 1

Library of Congress Cataloging-in-Publication Data

Simons, Robert.
  Control in an age of empowerment / Robert Simons.
    p. cm. – (Harvard business review classics)
  ISBN 978-1-4221-2672-1
  1. Span of control. 2. Management. I. Title.
  HD50.S56 2008
  658.4–dc22
                          2008017538

THE
HARVARD BUSINESS REVIEW
CLASSICS SERIES

Since 1922, *Harvard Business Review* has been a leading source of breakthrough ideas in management practice—many of which still speak to and influence us today. The HBR Classics series now offers you the opportunity to make these seminal pieces a part of your permanent management library. Each volume contains a groundbreaking idea that has shaped best practices and inspired countless managers around the world—and will change how you think about the business world today.

{ v }

CONTROL IN AN AGE OF EMPOWERMENT

A fundamental problem facing managers in the 1990s is how to exercise adequate control in organizations that demand flexibility, innovation, and creativity. Competitive businesses with demanding and informed customers must rely on employee initiative to seek out opportunities and respond to customers' needs. But pursuing some opportunities can expose businesses to excessive risk or invite behaviors that can damage a company's integrity.

Consider the spate of management control failures that have made headlines in the past several years: Kidder, Peabody & Company lost $350 million when a trader allegedly booked fictitious profits; Sears, Roebuck and Company took a $60 million charge against earnings after admitting that it recommended unnecessary repairs to customers in its automobile service business; Standard Chartered Bank was banned from trading on the Hong Kong stock market after being implicated in an improper share support scheme. The list goes on. In each case, employees broke through existing control mechanisms and jeopardized the franchise of the business. The cost to the companies—in damaged reputations, fines, business losses, missed opportunities, and diversion of man-

agement attention to deal with the crises—
was enormous.

How do senior managers protect their
companies from control failures when empowered employees are encouraged to rede-
fine how they go about doing their jobs?
How do managers ensure that subordinates
with an entrepreneurial flair do not put the
well-being of the business at risk? One solu-
tion is to go back to the fundamentals of control developed in the 1950s and 1960s for
machinelike bureaucracies. In that era, managers exercised control by telling people
how to do their jobs and monitoring them
with constant surveillance to guard against
surprises. Although this approach sounds
anachronistic for modern businesses, it is still
effective when standardization is critical for

efficiency and yield, such as on an assembly line; when the risk of theft of valuable assets is high, such as in a casino; or when quality and safety are essential to product performance, such as at a nuclear power plant.

However, in most organizations operating in dynamic and highly competitive markets, managers cannot spend all their time and effort making sure that everyone is doing what is expected. Nor is it realistic to think that managers can achieve control by simply hiring good people, aligning incentives, and hoping for the best. Instead, today's managers must encourage employees to initiate process improvements and new ways of responding to customers' needs–but in a controlled way.

Fortunately, the tools to reconcile the conflict between creativity and control are at hand. Most managers tend to define control narrowly—as measuring progress against plans to guarantee the predictable achievement of goals. Such diagnostic control systems are, however, only one ingredient of control. Three other levers are equally important in today's business environment: beliefs systems, boundary systems, and interactive control systems (see exhibits 1 and 2).

Each of the four control levers has a distinct purpose for managers attempting to harness the creativity of employees. Diagnostic control systems allow managers to ensure that important goals are being achieved efficiently and effectively. Beliefs systems empower individuals and encourage them to search for new opportunities. They communicate core values and inspire all participants to commit to the organization's purpose. Boundary systems establish the rules of the game and identify actions and pitfalls that employees must avoid. Interactive control systems enable top-level managers to focus on strategic uncertainties, to learn about threats and opportunities as competitive conditions change, and to respond proactively.

DIAGNOSTIC CONTROL SYSTEMS

Diagnostic control systems work like the dials on the control panel of an airplane cockpit, enabling the pilot to scan for signs of abnormal functioning and to keep critical performance variables within preset limits. Most businesses have come to rely on diagnostic control systems to help managers track the progress of individuals, departments, or production facilities toward strategically important goals. Managers use these systems to monitor goals and profitability, and to measure progress toward targets such as revenue growth and market share. Periodically, managers measure the outputs and compare them with preset standards of performance. Feedback allows management to adjust and fine-tune inputs and processes so that future outputs will more closely match goals.

But diagnostic control systems are not adequate to ensure effective control. In fact, they create pressures that can lead to control failures—even crises. Whether managers realize it or not, there are built-in dangers when empowered employees are held accountable for performance goals—especially for difficult ones—and then left to their own devices to achieve them. For example, Nordstrom, the upscale fashion retailer known for extraordinary customer service, recently found itself embroiled in a series of lawsuits and investigative reports related to its sales-per-hour performance-measurement system. Used to track the performance of its entrepreneurial salespeople, the system was designed to support the service orientation for which Nordstrom is famous. But without counterbalancing controls, the system created the potential for both exemplary customer service and abuse. Some employees claimed that first-line supervisors were pressuring them to underreport hours on the job in an attempt to boost sales per hour. Settling those claims cost Nordstrom more than $15 million.

I recently conducted a study of ten newly appointed chief executive officers to understand better how they used measurement and control systems to implement their agendas. Within the first months of taking charge, many of the new CEOs established demanding performance goals for division managers and increased the rewards and punishments associated with success and failure in achieving those goals. In response to the pressures, several division managers manipulated financial data by creating false accounting entries to enhance their reported performance. The managers were fired, but not before they had inflicted damage on their organizations. In one memorable case, a retail company had been making inventory and markdown decisions based on the falsified data, a practice that resulted in significant losses. These are not isolated incidents. The Big Six accounting firms have observed a substantial increase in errors and fraud over the past five years as organizations downsize and reduce the resources devoted to internal controls. With the elimination of many middle management jobs, basic internal controls, such as segregation of duties and independent oversight, have often been sacrificed.

One of the main purposes of diagnostic measurement systems is to eliminate the manager's burden of constant monitoring. Once goals are established and people have performance targets on which their rewards will be based, many managers believe they can move on to other issues, knowing that employees will be working diligently to meet the agreed-upon goals. Yet the potential for control failures as the performance bar is raised and employees' rewards are put at risk underscores the need for managers to think about the three other essential levers of control.

BELIEFS SYSTEMS

Companies have used beliefs systems for years in an effort to articulate the values and direction that senior managers want their employees to embrace. Typically, beliefs systems are concise, value-laden, and inspirational. They draw employees' attention to key tenets of the business: how the organization creates value ("Best Customer Service in the World"); the level of performance the organization strives for ("Pursuit of Excellence"); and how individuals are expected to manage both internal and external relationships ("Respect for the Individual").

Senior managers intentionally design beliefs systems to be broad enough to appeal to many different groups within an organization: salespeople, managers, production workers, and clerical personnel. Because they are broad, beliefs statements are often ridiculed for lacking substance. But this criticism overlooks the principal purpose of the statements: to inspire and promote commitment to an organization's core values. Still, the statements achieve their ends only if employees believe, by watching the actions of senior managers, that the company's stated beliefs represent deeply rooted values. If employees suspect that managers are going through the motions of the latest fad, cynicism will set in.

Indeed, some managers adopt missions and credos not out of any real commitment but because they seem fashionable. However, managers who use their missions as living documents—as part of a system to guide patterns of acceptable behavior—have discovered a powerful lever of control. At Johnson & Johnson, for example, senior managers meet regularly with subordinates throughout the company to review and reaffirm the beliefs recorded in J&J's long-standing credo, which articulates clearly and passionately the company's responsibilities to customers, employees, local communities, and stockholders. Managers throughout the organization recognize the value that senior managers place on the exercise and respond accordingly. When problems arise, such as when J&J faced the Tylenol crisis, the strong beliefs system embedded in its credo provided guidance regarding the types of solutions to search for.

In the past, a company's mission was usually understood without reference to core values or formal beliefs; employees knew that they worked for a bank or a telephone company or a company that made shock absorbers. However, businesses have become much more complex in recent years, making it more difficult for individuals to comprehend organizational purpose and direction. Moreover, in many businesses, downsizing and realignment have shattered strongly held assumptions about the values and foundations of businesses and their top-level managers. Employees no longer know whom to trust. At the same time, their expectations for meaningful careers have risen as education levels have increased. Without a formal beliefs system, employees in large, decentralized organizations often do not have a clear and consistent understanding of the core values of the business and their place within the business. In the absence of clearly articulated core values, they are often forced to make assumptions about what constitutes acceptable behavior in the many different, unpredictable circumstances they encounter.

Beliefs systems can also inspire employees to create new opportunities: they can motivate individuals to search for new ways of creating value. We all have a deep-seated need to contribute—to devote time and energy to worthwhile endeavors. But companies often make it difficult for employees to understand the larger purpose of their efforts or to see how they can add value in a way that can make a difference. Individuals want to understand the organization's purpose and how they can contribute, but senior managers must unleash this potential. Effective managers seek to inspire people throughout their organizations by actively communicating core values and missions. As top-level managers rely increasingly on empowered employees to generate new ideas and competitive advantage, participants from all parts of an organization need to understand as clearly as possible their company's purposes and mission.

Beliefs systems can augment diagnostic control systems to give today's managers greater amounts of control. But they are only part of the answer. Think of them as the yang of Chinese philosophy—the sun, the warmth, and the light. Opposing them are dark, cold boundaries—the yin—which represent the next lever of control.

BOUNDARY SYSTEMS

Boundary systems are based on a simple, yet profound, management principle that can be called the "power of negative thinking."[1] Ask yourself the question, If I want my employees to be creative and entrepreneurial, am I better off telling them what to do or telling them what *not* to do? The answer is the latter. Telling people what to do by establishing standard operating procedures and rule books discourages the initiative and creativity unleashed by empowered, entrepreneurial employees. Telling them what *not* to do allows innovation, but within clearly defined limits.

Unlike diagnostic control systems (which monitor critical performance outcomes) or beliefs systems (which communicate core values), boundary systems are stated in negative terms or as minimum standards. The boundaries in modern organizations, embedded in standards of ethical behavior and codes of conduct, are invariably written in terms of activities that are off-limits. They are an organization's brakes. Every business needs them, and, like racing cars, the fastest and most performance-oriented companies need the best brakes.

Human beings are inventive, and, when presented with new opportunities or challenging situations, they often search for ways to create value or overcome obstacles. But empowerment—fueled by inspiration and performance rewards—should never be interpreted as giving subordinates a blank check to do whatever they please. People generally want to do the right thing—to act ethically in accordance with established moral codes. But pressures to achieve superior results sometimes collide with stricter codes of behavior. Because of temptation or pressure in the workplace, individuals sometimes choose to bend the rules. As the recent problems at Kidder, Peabody and Salomon Brothers show, entrepreneurial individuals sometimes blur or misinterpret the line between acceptable and unacceptable behavior. At Salomon Brothers, a creative trader attempting to increase investment returns violated U.S. Treasury bidding rules and short-circuited existing controls; the aftermath of the scandal destroyed careers and impaired Salomon's franchise. Similar problems at Kidder, Peabody involving fictitious securities trades resulted in massive losses and ultimately led to the sale of the business. Clearly, the consequences of a misstep can be severe.

Boundary systems are especially critical in those businesses in which a reputation built on trust is a key competitive asset. A

well respected bank with a global franchise
states as a part of its business principles that
its three main assets are people, capital, and
reputation. Of all these, it notes, the last is
the most difficult to regain if impaired. To
guard against damage to its reputation, the
bank's code of conduct forbids individuals
both from developing client relationships in
"undesirable" industries, such as gambling
casinos, and from acting as intermediaries in
unfriendly takeovers, which senior managers
believe could undermine the perceived trust-
worthiness of the company.

   Large consulting firms like McKinsey &
Company and the Boston Consulting Group
routinely work with clients to analyze highly
proprietary strategic data. To ensure that

their reputations for integrity are never com-
promised, the firms enforce strict boundaries that forbid consultants to reveal
information—even the names of clients—to
anyone not employed by the firm, including
spouses. They also clearly state in their
codes of professional conduct that individuals must not misrepresent themselves when
attempting to gather competitive information on behalf of clients.

Unfortunately, the benefits of establishing
business conduct boundaries are not always
apparent to senior managers. Too often, they
learn the hard way. Many codes of conduct
are instituted only after a public scandal or
an internal investigation of questionable behavior. Over the years, General Electric has

instituted codes of business conduct that prohibit activities relating to improper payments, price fixing, and improper cost allocation on government contracts. Each of those codes was instituted after a major crisis impaired the integrity of the business. For instance, when GE was forced to suspend its $4.5 billion business as supplier to the U.S. government in 1985, CEO Jack Welch responded by strengthening internal controls and issuing a clear policy statement that forbade the behaviors that had landed GE in trouble: improper cost allocations on government contracts. Similarly, senior managers at Wall Street investment firms did not pay much attention to business conduct boundary systems until the disclosure of improper behavior by a small number of em-

ployees at Salomon Brothers nearly destroyed
the business. Again, senior managers at investment firms across the country scrambled
to install compliance systems to avoid a similar crisis in their own firms.

Effective managers anticipate the inevitable temptations and pressures that exist
within their organizations. They spell out
the rules of the game based on the risks in-
herent in their strategy and enforce them
clearly and unambiguously. Some behaviors
are never tolerated: the firing of the manager
who inflated his or her expense report by $50
is a familiar story in many organizations. On
the surface, the punishment may seem too
harsh for the crime, but the purpose of such
punishment is to signal clearly to all managers and employees that the consequences

of stepping over ethical boundaries are severe and nonnegotiable. As performance-oriented organizations grow and become more decentralized, the risks of failure increase. Managers must rely more and more on formal systems in order to ensure that the boundaries are communicated and understood.

Not all boundaries concern standards of ethical conduct. Strategic boundaries focus on ensuring that people steer clear of opportunities that could diminish the business's competitive position. A large computer company, for example, uses its strategic planning process to segregate its product and market opportunities into what managers call *green space* and *red space*. Green space is the acceptable domain for new initiatives. Red space represents products and markets in which senior managers have decided they do not want to pursue new opportunities, although the organization could compete in those products and markets given its competencies. A British relief organization uses a similar system to monitor strategic boundaries; it maintains a *gray list* of companies whose contributions it will neither solicit nor accept. Managers at Automatic Data Processing (ADP) use a strategic boundary list that delineates the types of business opportunities that managers must avoid. The guidelines provide ADP managers with clarity and focus. This technique has contributed to 133 consecutive quarters of double-digit growth in earnings per share–a record unmatched by any other company traded on the New York Stock Exchange.

Working together, boundary systems and beliefs systems are the yin and yang that together create a dynamic tension. The warm, positive, inspirational beliefs are a foil to the dark, cold constraints. The result is a dynamic tension between commitment and punishment. Together, these systems transform limitless opportunity into a focused domain that employees and managers are encouraged to exploit actively. In combination, they establish direction, motivate and inspire, and protect against potentially damaging opportunistic behavior.

INTERACTIVE CONTROL SYSTEMS

When organizations are small, key managers and employees can sit around the same table and informally explore the impact of emerging threats and opportunities. But as organizations grow larger and senior managers have less and less personal contact with people throughout the organization, new formal systems must be created to share emerging information and to harness the creativity that often leads to new products, line extensions, processes, and even markets. Unfortunately, diagnostic control systems, which highlight shortfalls against plans, won't suffice. Instead, senior managers need sensing systems more like the ones used by the National Weather Service. Ground stations all over the country monitor temperature, barometric pressure, relative humidity, cloud cover, wind direction and velocity, and precipitation. Balloons and satellites provide additional data. These data are monitored continuously from a central location in an effort to identify patterns of change.

Managers need similar scanning mechanisms. Like weather-tracking systems, interactive control systems are the formal information systems that managers use to involve themselves regularly and personally in the decisions of subordinates. These systems are generally simple to understand. Through them, senior managers participate in the decisions of subordinates and focus organizational attention and learning on key strategic issues.

Making a control system interactive invariably demands attention from participants throughout the business. At Pepsico, for example, the weekly release of new Nielsen market-share numbers creates a flurry of activity as 60 or 70 people throughout the organization begin working on the data in anticipation of the inevitable scrutiny and queries of senior management. Senior managers schedule weekly meetings to discuss the new Nielsen information, to challenge subordinates to explain the meaning of changed circumstances, and to review action plans that subordinates have developed to react to problems and opportunities.

Interactive control systems have four characteristics that set them apart from diagnostic control systems. First, they focus on constantly changing information that top-level managers have identified as potentially strategic. Second, the information is significant enough to demand frequent and regular attention from operating managers at all levels of the organization. Third, the data generated by the interactive system are best interpreted and discussed in face-to-face meetings of superiors, subordinates, and peers. Fourth, the interactive control system is a catalyst for an ongoing debate about underlying data, assumptions, and action plans.

Interactive control systems track the strategic uncertainties that keep senior managers awake at night—the shocks to the business that could undermine their assumptions about the future and the way they have chosen to compete. Depending on the business, these uncertainties might relate to changes in technology, customers' tastes, government regulation, and industry competition. Because interactive control systems are designed to gather information that might challenge visions of the future, they are, by definition, hot buttons for senior managers.

A senior manager's decision to use a specific control system interactively—in other words, to invest time and attention in face-to-face meetings to review new information—sends a clear signal to the organization about what's important. Through the dialogue and debate that surround the interactive process, new strategies often emerge. Consider the case of a well-known hospital supply company. The company is a low-cost producer, supplying disposable hospital products for intravenous drug delivery such as plasma containers, tubing, and syringes. Even though efficiency, quality, and cost control are important competencies, these concerns do not keep managers awake at night. (They are well understood and can be managed effectively with diagnostic control systems.) Instead, senior managers worry that technological breakthroughs will undermine their ability to deliver products valued by the market. Accordingly, they use a project management system interactively to focus organizational attention on a dozen or so emerging technological issues. Senior managers meet monthly for several days to debate the impact of technologies—introduced by competitors or in related industries, or developed in-house—on their business.

These meetings become intense as the managers challenge one another to assess the impact of new information and develop responses. From this dialogue, new strategies emerge.

Senior managers at *USA Today*, Gannett Company's daily newspaper, use a similar process to review information contained in a simple package of reports delivered each Friday. Three weekly reports give senior managers a picture of how they have done in the previous week and what conditions lie ahead for the upcoming few weeks. The data in the Friday packet range from year-to-date figures to daily and account-specific information. These data provide insight into changing industry conditions and the advertising strategies of key customers. They allow managers to look at the big picture and provide enough detail to identify specific vulnerabilities, opportunities, and the source of any problems that require proactive responses.

Each week, senior managers at *USA Today* schedule intensive face-to-face meetings with key subordinates to analyze and interpret the report data. Among the regular topics of discussion and debate are advertising volume against plan, committed future volume by issue, and new business by type of client. In addition to looking for unexpected shortfalls, managers also look for unexpected successes. From these meetings, significant innovations have been proposed to deal with unanticipated downturns and to capitalize on unanticipated opportunities. Innovations have included launching a new market-survey service for automotive clients, introducing fractional-page color advertising, selling exclusive inserts dedicated to specific customers and products, and using circulation salespeople to sell ad space in regional locations.

Of course, managers in other businesses choose different kinds of control systems to use interactively depending on the strategic uncertainties associated with their business strategies. For example, Johnson & Johnson uses its profit-planning system interactively to focus attention on the development and protection of innovative products in its various markets. Managers periodically reestimate the predicted effects of competitive tactics and new product rollouts on their profit plans for the current and the following year. The recurring questions posed by managers are: What has changed since our last forecast? Why? What are we going to do about it? The results are new ideas and action plans.

BALANCING EMPOWERMENT AND CONTROL

Effective managers empower their organizations because they believe in the innate potential of people to innovate and add value. For instance, the reason Nordstrom salespeople provide exceptional customer service is that they are selected and trained to act entrepreneurially. In turn, they have the freedom and motivation to tailor their service to each customer's needs. To unleash this type of potential, senior managers must give up control over many kinds of decisions and allow employees at lower levels of the organization to act independently. Good managers work constantly to help employees rise to their potential. In small organizations, managers do this informally. While eating or traveling together, they communicate core values and missions, the rules of the game, and current targets—and they learn about significant changes. As companies become larger, more decentralized, and geographically dispersed, senior managers are no longer in constant contact with all the employees who will identify and respond to emerging problems and opportunities. Nonetheless, the guiding principles of communication and control are every bit as important.

A large international construction company respected for its quality and customer service provides a clear illustration of how the control levers support one another. The company has more than 25 offices in the United States and abroad; as a result, project managers and employees make multimillion-dollar decisions far from the company's top-level managers. The senior managers who set the company's overall direction and strategy ensure that they have adequate control of their far-flung operations by using all four levers of control.

To communicate core values, they rely on a beliefs system. The company's widely circu-

lated credo refers to the importance of re-
sponsibility, of collective pride in engineering
quality, of financial success, and of integrity.
It concludes with an overall objective handed
down by the founder: "To be the best."

These inspirational beliefs are offset by
clear boundaries. Managers are forbidden,
for example, to work in certain countries
where facilitating payments and bribes are
required to do business, because these sorts
of actions jeopardize the company's belief
in integrity. The company also maintains a
turkey list to communicate to managers the
types of projects that the company has learned
are not profitable and should be avoided.
(For example, senior managers have learned
from bitter experience to steer clear of
sewage-disposal-plant construction.) The

list is adjusted from time to time as managers learn where their competencies lie and where they don't.

Managers gain still more control by using a variety of diagnostic controls—among them profit plans, budgets, and goals and objectives. These control systems do not require very much attention from senior management other than the time spent setting annual goals and monitoring exceptions to see that events unfold according to plan. One control system, however, is used interactively. The project management system focuses attention on the strategic uncertainties that managers want everyone to monitor: the company's reputation in the trade, the shifting perceptions of customers, and the ideal skill mix required in various project teams. The new data are used as a catalyst to force regular face-to-face discussions in which managers share information and attempt to develop better ways to customize their services and adjust their strategies in a changing market.

Collectively, these four levers of control set in motion powerful forces that reinforce one another. As organizations become more complex, managers will inevitably deal with increasing opportunity and competitive forces and decreasing time and attention. By using the control levers effectively, managers can be confident that the benefits of innovation and creativity are not achieved at the expense of control.

EXHIBIT 1

Harness Employees' Creativity with the Four Levers of Control

Potential	Organizational Blocks	Managerial Solution	Control Lever
To contribute	Uncertainty about purpose	Communicate core values and mission	Beliefs systems
To do right	Pressure or temptation	Specify and enforce rules of the game	Boundary systems
To achieve	Lack of focus or of resources	Build and support clear targets	Diagnostic control systems
To create	Lack of opportunity or fear of risk	Open organizational dialogue to encourage learning	Interactive control systems

EXHIBIT 2

Renew strategy with the four levers of control

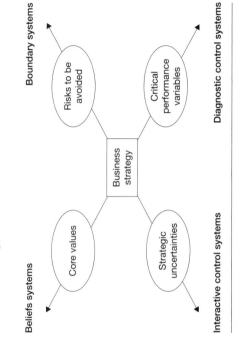

NOTES

1. My colleague, Professor Charles Christenson, coined this term in a 1972 Harvard Business School working paper.

ABOUT THE AUTHOR

Robert Simons is the Charles M. Williams Professor of Business Administration and chairman of Harvard's Advanced Management Program at Harvard Business School in Boston, Massachusetts. His book *Levers of Organization Design* was published by Harvard Business Press in 2005.

ALSO BY THIS AUTHOR

Harvard Business Press Books

Levers of Organization Design: How Managers Use Accountability Systems for Greater Performance and Commitment

Levers of Control: How Managers Use Innovative Control Systems to Drive Strategic Renewal

Harvard Business Review Articles

"Designing High Performance Jobs"

"How Risky is Your Company"

"How High is Your Return on Management"
with Antonio Davila

Harvard Business Cases

"Nordstrom: Dissension in the Ranks?"
with Hilary A. Weston

"Codman & Shurtleff, Inc.: Planning and
Control System"

"Polysar Ltd."

"Citibank: Performance Evaluation"
with Antonio Davila

Article Summary

The Idea in Brief

When we praise creative employees, we generally don't have in mind the Kidder, Peabody trader who booked fictitious profits and ultimately cost the company $350 million.

On the one hand, employee initiative is more important than ever. Failure to nurture innovation and empower employees can lead to stagnation. But on the other hand, there is no shortage of cases where the zeal of an individual employee has crossed the line into harmful behavior. Failure to control employees appropriately, therefore, can lead to disaster: business losses, civil or criminal penalties, and perhaps most important, loss of reputation.

This dilemma doesn't require an either/or decision. Managers can encourage innovation among employees while ensuring adequate control by using four powerful management systems or "levers."

The Idea at Work

How can you protect your company while promoting entrepreneurial flair? Think of control as embodying four distinct levers:

- *Diagnostic control systems* are the traditional monitors of critical performance outcomes such as costs and revenues. But holding employees accountable for performance without having other monitoring systems in place can cause problems.

Example: Nordstrom used diagnostic systems to track the performance of its sales force. But then some employees brought a lawsuit claiming that supervisors were pressuring them to under-report their hours on the job, so sales per hour would look better. Settling the claim cost Nordstrom more than $15 million.

- *Belief systems* encompass the company's values, mission, and other statements of philosophy. When managers dismiss such beliefs, employees become cynical. However, managers who "walk the talk" and exemplify appropriate behavior have a powerful lever of control over employee actions. For example, Johnson & Johnson's regular meetings to reaffirm its business credo proved invaluable in the search for solutions during the Tylenol crisis.

- *Boundary systems* are based on the "power of negative thinking." If you want employees to be creative, don't tell them what to do— tell them what *not* to do. Setting boundaries means establishing the rules of the game.

  Example: A large computer maker segregates business opportunities into green space—marketing segments where employees are encourged to innovate—and red space—those markets the company has decided not to pursue because they may dilute its competitive position.

- *Interactive control systems* are especially important as organizations grow larger and senior managers have less personal contact with employees. Using the interactive lever means sharing market information and encouraging creative responses while helping people avoid pitfalls. At *USA Today*, senior managers responsible for advertising revenue meet weekly with key subordinates to go over a packet of data on year-to-date and other measures of ad performance.

Diagnostic systems represent the traditional approach of measuring progress toward goals. The belief, boundary, and interactive systems add the elements needed to respond appropriately and profitably to today's markets. When used in concert, these four levers can give you the control you need without sacrificing the flexibility and creativity you can't do without.